What Do I Do About Hitting?!

What Do I Do About Hitting?!

Understanding and learning to manage childhood
rage, anger and frustration

Another book of tips for parents who have
children with special needs

by

Martha Kate Downey

Edited by Anne Gerard Staton

Books by MK
(817) 267-8563
http://www.mkdowney.com

Martha Kate Downey
mdo651@airmail.net

First Edition
ISBN 0-9742421-0-1

Printed and Bound in United States of America

CONTENTS

To Kate,
who as a small child,
taught me through action -
and as an adult,
teaches others through courage

Acknowledgments

For all those parents who seek answers and don't give up,

For sons who have compassion,

For my mother,
Mel Ruth Aikin and my teacher, Sister Margaret Basso
who inspire me with their wisdom,

For my friends,
Anne Staton, Stephen Shore and Dorothy O'Daniel,
who graciously accepted my pleas,

And, of course, for my co-conspirator, Dennis Downey,
who supports unceasingly,

I give thanks.

Foreword

By Stephen Shore

Author of <u>Beyond the Wall: Personal Experiences with Autism and Asperger Syndrome</u>

What Do I Do About Hitting?! makes an important contribution to the body of autism spectrum literature because it deals with one of the most difficult and unpredictable emotions that people with autism need to handle, "anger." As a person diagnosed with strong autistic tendencies in 1964, it is clear to me that Martha Kate understands the importance of strong parental support for guiding autistic children through a confusing environment. Things we take for granted such as how to socialize, communicate, gauge the forcefulness of one's touch, distinguish one emotion from another, or even conceive the passage of time were a complete mystery for Martha Kate's daughter, Kate. Fortunately, Kate had her mom to help solve these areas of confusion, reducing the high levels of frustration, anxiety and tension that are so common in people with autism.

Having worked with many families whose children are on the autism spectrum, it is clear to me that Martha Kate expresses a rare talent for reaching inside her daughter's world as she guides her through childhood, the turbulent teen years and on to adulthood. Martha Kate engages the reader, and not only brings him into the world of her daughter, but also into the life of a mother parenting a daughter on the autism spectrum.

One part of the book is especially helpful: making sense of the causes and interventions for child tantrums, which are all too common for those with autism. Often one of the most feared childhood behaviors, Martha Kate implores us to find the cause of these challenging episodes in order to manage them when they do occur, or even better, keep the frustration from escalating past the "rumbling" stage. One example of preventive medicine for tantrums is some simple breathing exercises that would be helpful to all of us for reducing tension. Additionally, parents can pick and choose from the many other useful "stress relievers" and parenting tips for decreasing anxiety outlined toward the end of the book.

Focusing on parents, teachers and others who come into contact with those on the autism spectrum, Martha Kate's writing style makes the reader feel as if he is conversing with a wise, and at the same time, sympathetic and understanding parent.

One of the most important lessons Martha Kate teaches us is that the child is the greatest teacher. Our challenge, be it as a parent, teacher, professional or friend, is to learn how to listen to that child; to let go of our desire to control in favor of providing guidance that paves the way toward a productive and fulfilling life. Through actions and/or words, the child will inform you as to his needs and preferences.

Your time with Martha Kate will be an informative and enlightening experience. While Martha Kate is an author, speaker and educator, it is clear that her priorities are in the right place for any parent...she is mainly Mom.

Introduction

Anger is a part of life. Learning how to react to anger in a constructive way is a very difficult, yet necessary, skill to master. Kids need to know how to show frustration without hurting themselves, other people or anyone's property.

Managing feelings of frustration, anger and rage are challenging components of growing up for any child, but these feelings are especially difficult to manage when the ways of the world are confusing, scary or painful. This book will help the parent or caregiver better understand the frustrations that a child with special challenges encounters in a "neurologically typical" world.

The book also discusses major issues that create difficulties and lead to stress for the older child or teenager. Topics such as decision-making, control, *sensory integration or defensiveness, and the inability to feel subtleties of anxiety, which lead to full-fledged rage, are considered. When parents teach strategies for handling individual frustrations in healthy ways, they prepare their young children to skillfully manage more complex ones later on. The child who learns about healthy anger management is much less likely to become a teen or an adult who experiences overwhelming rage or depression.

Early anger management is so very important! We hope our experiences through the years with Kate, our daughter who has autism, will provide insights to other parents who have a child with special challenges. She was a very confused young child, yet she is now a very happy, assured young adult with the courage to share her experiences for the benefit of others.

11

A private word with other parents...

I wrote this book as a means of encouragement for other parents who have children with exceptional challenges. I remember how completely overwhelmed my husband and I felt as we tried to help Kate fit better into the world.

Kate had some good doctors and some very good teachers, but most didn't offer help to us as a family. It wasn't even their jobs to do that. It was frustrating when I realized that the diagnostic specialists couldn't tell me how to get through a day, and the teachers just wanted the kid fixed and coming to school in a frame of mind ready to learn, but neither group was equipped to advise us about accomplishing those tasks.

As parents, we so often become angry with the messengers (doctors or educators) because they give us information we don't know what to do with. We also resented being asked if we had questions, just as they were clearly showing us the door. Generally, we have many questions...but not at the moment when we first hear the doctor pronounce a diagnosis for our child. When the diagnosis is an uncommon one, or one we are fearful to accept, we feel overwhelmed and utterly lacking in personal resources to handle the situation. The sad thing is, it isn't the doctor's responsibility to tell you how to live with this child. A doctor's job is to diagnose and describe the condition, not suggest how to change your child's habits. He won't tell you what to do when your kid repeatedly takes all the books off the shelves, or calls 911 in the middle of the night because he's discovered that someone will answer the phone at that hour. Nor can they tell you how to get a family relative to become more accepting of your exceptionally * "flavorful" child.

I desperately needed to know how to live. I needed to know how to keep our family safe and remain concerned with the needs of all, not just focused on the needs of one. I knew a psychologist might be very helpful, but I also knew we needed more than just a few hour's worth of help because our needs continued to grow and change. We needed a new way of living.

I thought I needed to know how to handle every situation. Aren't all Moms and Dads supposed to know how to care for their children? Aren't we expected to control their behavior? Aren't we supposed to know why they are crying and be able to kiss it and make it better? It wasn't getting better, and I felt like a failure as Kate's mom..

I was very lucky, though. I have a friend who does some counseling. She's a Catholic nun, whom I always thought needed "nun lessons." She deals with real life issues, in real language, and doesn't shy from hard, unanswerable questions. She didn't tell me how to manage my family; she just helped me see that we were *all* going to be all right. She took the urgency out of the situation and helped me get a larger picture of my role as a mother and of Kate's life situation. She helped me realize that I needed less control than expected but also had more control than I was aware of. She helped me embrace my family for all it is, and see our autistic daughter as part of us, not all of us! She assured me that if I had the parenting skills to keep Kate healthy and okay today, she would also be healthy and okay tomorrow.

I want to share with you the most important lesson Sister Margaret taught me: Kate would be the teacher and I, the student. I thought my job as Mom was to lead the way, but I didn't have any idea where to go or how to get there. Sister Margaret taught me to pay attention... really, really pay attention to Kate. She said Kate would tell us how to help her.

13

Strange, I know, but that's exactly how it worked out. I found myself doing less fretting and more observing of her actions, her patterns, her joys, and her fears. When I was in a crowd, I began paying more attention to her and less to the reactions of others. (I won't go into all the behaviors that concerned us...if you're reading this book, you know them!) As I studied Kate, I learned how to begin to teach her, and she came to trust me. My curiosity about her world and her tenaciousness to live her life, *her way*, was an essential element to discovering her needs and talents. Kate's proved to be a wonderful, motivating teacher, and we have been eager, though sometimes exhausted students. Sister Margaret's lessons have taken us on an exciting, challenging and fruitful journey. Contrary to my earlier fears, we have discovered we are a healthier, happier family because of Kate, not in spite of her!

This is not to say we didn't have some very challenging years. The ages of seven and eight were extremely difficult ones. Those are the years when our kids become more self-aware and start to understand cause/effect and control issues. Kate's anger, which could often be intense, was part of our daily life. It made it difficult to go places as a family. It caused our older son to ask if I would be safe if he went on to school, as I was the primary target for her aggression. (Children with special challenges often target their physical aggression on those persons they trust most. They expect these people to help them cope and believe it unlikely that those chosen few will become alienated even after suffering their hostility. These children experience uncontrolled anger born of confusion and *sensorial issues, but they don't intentionally fight the trusted person; they simply are not aware of alternate methods to get rid of their anger.) At any rate, it was hard and scary to live with this child who was so totally out of my control.

14

Fortunately, by the time Kate was an early adolescent we had had a few years to practice learning from her. We also found a doctor who understood *obsessive-compulsive disorder and was aware of medications that could ease some of Kate's symptoms. The medications enabled Kate to concentrate on acquiring new skills for managing her feelings and actions. She was ready to start learning new methods for making decisions and taking control. What followed were two years of growth for us all. Those two years were hard, yet enlightening ones. With Kate's guidance and strength we began to experience hope! What a gift that is, HOPE. Without it we cannot learn.

Teen years came, along with new issues and more changes, but by that time we were all more skilled at relaxing and learning from one another. We had learned that we could and would handle the changes. (To be honest, there were times of despair when she'd slide back into old and less productive behaviors.) She's now 21 years old, and she manages anger more effectively than many adults without neurological challenges! Her outlook is confident and positive, and she knows she has a secure place both in her world and ours. Like us all, she sometimes gets mildly angry and occasionally offers a less than "lady-like" expletive, but I am usually the only one who hears her briefly muttered outburst. I must admit that uttering a curse word is sometimes just what the doctor ordered…say it, get it out, move on. Better than bopping your mother!

So here's to you, dear parents. You'll make it through these scary years because you have hope, that element that turns a stumbling block into a stepping-stone. You're searching for answers and have the determination to live peacefully together.

Congratulations, guys! You're surviving…. Onward and upward!

15

Fragile!
Handle me with care

I can hear the falling dew drops
as they land upon the grass.
I can hear the turtles' footsteps
go around me as they pass.

I can see the shades of every hue
and cringe, when as they sometimes do
not blend or compliment, so what
I see is palette true.

I can feel the glaring brightness
of the lights that burn at night,
and can only tightly shut my eyes
against their hurtful sight.

If only we could clothe ourselves
with layers thick, not thin,
that would only let the right amount
of worldly senses in.

For even when you try to hug
me gently and with care,
your touch is often so much more
of comfort I can bear.

The lights, the smells, the touch, the taste
assault me everyday.
I wish that just for one short time
my sense would go away!

by Martha Kate Downey
copyright 1999 *TAP DANCING in the night*

Why is she hitting? Understanding the confusion of a young child's world (ages 3-6 years)

Such a beautiful baby was our daughter, Kate. Her body would mold into mine when I held her. Never one that strained to get loose, she was happy for the holding. Kate was laid back, a quiet baby with a peaches and cream complexion, bright eyes, and complacent nature. Yet her sleep patterns were *erratic. Sometimes she would sleep so soundly you could not arouse her, but when she would awaken in the middle of the night she could not be calm enough to settle back down to sleep. She was either all the way on (and awake) or all the way off (and asleep). She slept best on her daddy's chest. Hearing his heartbeat was a soothing and calming thing for her. It seemed to provide a singleness of sound that allowed her mind to focus enough to fall asleep. (Now she makes a monotone hum when she's concentrating, and I've wondered if that provides the same comfort and focus as her father's heart beat.)

She loved playing with bits of fabric and trim and was fascinated by her ceiling fan. But then... time for school! My sweet child hit preschool age, and she never stopped moving. What happened?! Why was she hitting, biting, kicking or pinching?

As a young child, Kate had great difficulty participating in a group or even in a one-to-one relationship with another child. She was in a three-year-old preschool class at our church, and within a few days she had trained the other children to be afraid of her.

Kate was darling: small, happy, but completely bewildered by the other children. The primary way she made contact was to hit them. She also would snatch their toys, bite them, etc. Had Kate turned into a monster? Of course not, but the classroom

18

setting, busy with bright colors and squeals of small children, was beyond her realm of comfort and understanding. Poor Kate, we had no idea what we had done to her! The class, designed to be a fun experience and teach socialization to young children, simply didn't work for her. Only after her diagnosis of autism did we begin to understand what was going on in her small world.

1. Kate saw the school kids and wanted them to play with her. At home, she had a brother, seven years older and large in stature. Kate, being unusually small, wanted to find a way to come into his world. Unfortunately, her language and social skills were extremely limited (although her ability to mimic sounds and speech was amazing!) Her big brother, David, fascinated Kate, but her lack of useful language and social awareness forced her to communicate the only way she knew how…physically. Kate lacked the sensory development to monitor the strength of her touch and had become accustomed to hitting David with unnecessary force. Was she angry with him? No, not at all. She just wanted to interact with him in some way, so he became a punching bag for her. Our instructions to Kate, "Just pat David," were not successful, and she would strike him quickly and unexpectedly. Unfortunately, he wouldn't try to stop her. Afraid of hurting her, he even refused to restrain her. We encouraged David to use words and say, "Stop that, now!" but to no avail. Poor David, always willing to let the other guy hurt him rather than inflict injury. Sadly, those habits went into the preschool classroom with Kate. This was a major issue because her classmates' bodies were also small. The children were frightened, and neither the teachers nor the parents were crazy about Kate's aggression.

Physical Communication

2. Part of Kate's aggression was a reaction to stress. If she felt overwhelmed by new sounds, smells, faces or directions she didn't understand, she would lash out at the child nearest her. (Oops, wrong response, Kate.) But we had no accurate diagnosis at that time and had simply been told she was "hyperactive." Although we attended the church where Kate was enrolled, and she already knew some of the children in her class, the preschool program was unfamiliar to her. It was filled with new experiences and obstacles that Kate didn't understand. She couldn't control her surroundings and was always in a highly excitable state. Kate's teacher was very gifted, but it was impossible for her to keep the room appropriately stimulated for all the children. If the room was calm enough for Kate, it was not developmentally stimulating enough for the other children. With too much light, noise, movement and people, a wild Kate was a certainty! She gave new meaning to the word "hyperactive"!

3. Kate also experienced sensory defensiveness. This is a problem for many kids who have *autism spectrum disorders (ASD). Sensory defensiveness varies in severity along a spectrum. An example of a mild reaction could be a child exhibiting rage for a short period of time over some insignificant or "unfixable" situation, such as being told to take a shower. The severest form, which our daughter does not exhibit, might manifest itself in prolonged screaming (lasting hours) with physical assaults on those unwise or unwary enough to get too close. Often the reaction to external stimuli could appear as a behavioral tantrum. These are not tantrums; they are physical reactions to intense sensations.

Physical reaction

4. Additionally, Kate had poor language and visual perception skills. She was very verbal, so her disability was hidden from her teachers and us. Now we know that most of her speech was just mimed behavior (*echolalia). She didn't know what she was saying and usually had little idea of what others were saying. It took a good speech therapist to finally discover that bit of information. Another therapist suggested that Kate was also having spatial difficulties (we were having tremendous problems with Kate wandering out of her yard). The therapist suggested that I let Kate take me by the hand and show me where her yard was. Imagine my astonishment when she took me all over the neighborhood giving me a tour of her yard! In this instance, Kate's difficulty with language was combined with her challenges involving visual perception.

5. As I mentioned earlier, Kate had no judgment about her touch. Never intending to hurt another person, she would often pat someone with a WHOP! (Even now as a young adult, she sometimes has difficulty monitoring her strength when playing with someone.) This inability to discern nuances of touch gave her a very high tolerance for pain. She simply couldn't feel differences in the degree or strength of a sensation.

6. Kate's inability to distinguish physical feelings affected her perception of inner feelings as well. Some emotions were felt strongly, but others very little. It appeared as though she didn't care when actually that was not the case.

7. Kate couldn't discriminate between one emotion and another. Anger, excitement and joy were all the same to her. Her response to any feeling was to physically react...often by biting, kicking or hitting the child nearest her. Those preschool kids remained her friends; however, they liked her best from a distance. Kate was lucky because the children's parents understood something unusual was going on. They were quite tolerant, but I'm sure they cautioned their children to stay out of her target range!

8. Kate also had no time concept, so I'm sure she was bewildered any time the activity would change, or if it was mentioned that something unusual would happen later. Not understanding the "plan" was terribly frustrating.

Kate was not ready for a classroom full of students; nor were they ready for her! Unfortunately, I knew so little about what was happening. Even though the social worker in me just "felt" as though autism might be present, the doctors didn't suggest (or wouldn't acknowledge) the possibility because "she is so verbal." Never mind that her speech was so rapid no one could understand it. Never mind that it was so disjointed a person had to spend the day with her to know what she was saying. Her description of her day, as told to her father, could have been, "Red, dog, shoe, park, David, couch." It meant that she had lost her red shoe and couldn't go to the park until she found it. David finally found her shoes under the couch, where the dog had probably put them.

No wonder this child was confused and frustrated ...as were we!

Conversation between
Kate   and the   school secretary

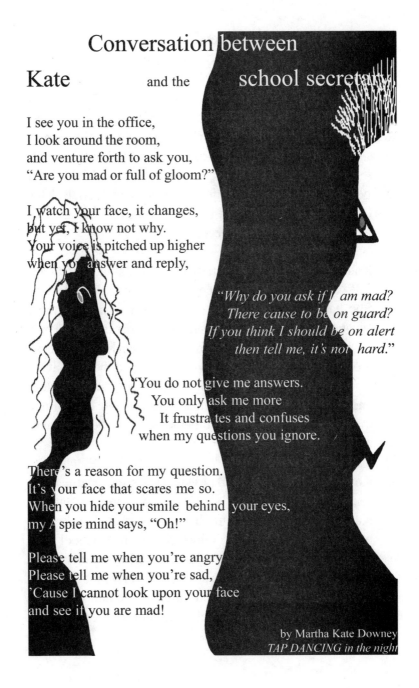

I see you in the office,
I look around the room,
and venture forth to ask you,
"Are you mad or full of gloom?"

I watch your face, it changes,
but yet, I know not why.
Your voice is pitched up higher
when you answer and reply,

"Why do you ask if I am mad?
There cause to be on guard?
If you think I should be on alert
then tell me, it's not hard."

"You do not give me answers.
You only ask me more
It frustrates and confuses
when my questions you ignore.

There's a reason for my question.
It's your face that scares me so.
When you hide your smile behind your eyes,
my A spie mind says, "Oh!"

Please tell me when you're angry
Please tell me when you're sad,
'Cause I cannot look upon your face
and see if you are mad!

by Martha Kate Downey
TAP DANCING in the night

23

Why is she so frustrated?
Children's frustrations (ages 6-12 years)

As Kate grew older, school became very trying for us all. So many things were not understood, and expectations from classmates and teachers, as well as her own, were not the same. Those conflicting expectations contributed to the building of anger and pent up anxieties. In addition to her preschool goals, Kate had to confront numerous new behavioral and social issues that arose during her elementary years.

1. Kate had many more opportunities, but her ability to practice self-control had not kept pace with her expanding interests. She had not been able to successfully manage simple situations in the past, so increasing the number and complexity of situations was not only confusing for her, but also caused anxiety. (Guess you know what happened then. WHOP! Back to hitting, biting, kicking...except now she was older and Mom was generally the nearest target. She had learned that she couldn't beat up on other kids, so this behavior was more limited to family.)

2. Kate's self-care skills and physical stamina became more important as her social and scholastic environments changed. Kate was still not sleeping through the night, so she was often tired during the day. Older kids in grade school were not taking naps, but Kate lacked the ability to stay awake and on track throughout the day. Some early motor control skills were not yet mastered either. Kate had difficulty participating in the games that other children were playing, making her more of an outcast.

3. The school setting was bigger, with more stimulation and more kids, but unfortunately, had less monitoring. Consequently, the potential for high anxiety, confusion and feeling overwhelmed was also greater.

4. Because she was now out of the home more, Kate was experiencing greater insight into society and her own expectations. Kate was discovering that the world measured a person's worth by arbitrary scales, values and ability to perform. This was scary because Kate didn't understand the value system nor could she perform many of skills that were desired.

5. What some students see as a reward or incentive, others might view differently. A class party could be fun for some, but for those with severe sensory defensiveness a party could be perceived as punishment.

6. Many times kids with autism see things as black or white, right or wrong, good or bad. They are unable to accept gray areas of thought, action and behavior. Unfortunately, this all-or-nothing attitude carries over into their work or personal expectations. Debilitating perfectionism in autistic children is a common problem. One interesting point regarding perfectionism is that it's incredibly subjective. Your child's idea of perfection may not be your perspective at all. It's difficult to convince another person to alter his definition of acceptable work.

7. Kate's reading skills were much improved, but her comprehension skills had not kept pace. The same discrepancy existed in speech as well; Kate couldn't always demonstrate understanding of what she had said or what she had heard. She had some verbal skills, but not enough understanding of language and pragmatics for clear communication to take place. It became a problem, both socially and scholastically. The listener was not always aware that her wide expressive vocabulary was often used inappropriately or gave erroneous information. We all thought she understood many things that she didn't grasp at all!

8. Kate was becoming more self-aware, but lacked the ability to express her feelings clearly or monitor their strength. The autism caused language delays that made it very difficult for her to state frustrations and emotions, or even identify what she was feeling. Her ability to perceive and/or avoid approaching anger was also very limited. She was learning to feel regret and guilt, but was unable to express it appropriately or change behavior. Kate loved me, so she had to deal with regret after she had hit me, etc. She didn't know how to verbally express her regret or change the antecedent behavior.

9. Diet was also a growing factor in her expanding world, and it greatly affected her behavior. It was important that she eat and drink those foods that helped her function best, especially during times when she was more likely to have difficulties in social settings. The more Kate participated in public outings, the greater her opportunity was to make poor food choices.

By the way, *Dexedrine's effectiveness is greatly reduced by ascorbic acid (Vitamin C). If you take morning meds, which include Dexedrine, followed by orange juice...you might as well pour it down the drain! For years I couldn't figure out why her behavior would change from day to day!

Kids seem to have much anger between the ages of seven and nine. When social maturity stagnates and children don't improve their ability to handle frustrations acceptably, there is increasing potential for more serious injuries and legal ramifications. I have known kids with similar characteristics as Kate's become really angry, aggressive and abusive teens. It's best to teach anger management when a child is still relatively easy to control (small body, no assault charges, role models available). Left unmanaged, the anger is likely to escalate and ultimately cause school officials or the judicial system to mete out discipline, rather than loving parents.

half poem: My Garden
- Michael Christensen

Our self, or our character,
is like a garden.
God created a beautiful garden
in each of us,
he made each garden unique and special,
each one containing a variety species which
are one of a kind,
so that we could admire each others
gardens,
each for its own unique beauty and special
magic.
Before I went to Kindergarten,
it was just us three -
my parents and me -
Nobody cared if my garden did not look the
same as others,
because that is how it was intended to be.
No one ever would have thought
that anything is wrong,
because my garden with its unique, special
magic
brought us happiness and love.
Alas, when I went to Kindergarten,
everything changed -

The Kindergarten teachers invaded my
garden,
they saw flowers here, a tree there,
which they had never seen before!
So they decided to go home and get a
shovel,
so they could dig up and destroy all my
beautiful flowers,
just to be able to plant ordinary ones in their
place!!

When the teacher began to stick her shovel
in the ground
and I saw she was up to NO GOOD,
I quickly sent a bunch of poisonous snakes
to scare her away
and to save my precious flowers.
I put up large walls
to protect my garden
I put up fierce guard-dogs, posted brutal
soldiers,
- to protect my garden
They said I was aggressive, mean,
dangerous, nasty, rude, etc.
But it wasn't a question
of what I was -
It was a question of what I wasn't:

I wasn't showing myself, my real garden.
But wouldn't it be safe
to let people who appreciate - who don't
want to destroy or change it -
Into my garden?
Dear Mom, dear Dad, dear Family,
why don't you come into the garden?
I'll take away the brutal soldier and the fierce
guard-dog,
I'll unlock the gate for you.

Do you think, perhaps, that I could dare
to leave the door slightly ajar for Juliana
and tell her:
You have already caught a glimpse of my
garden when I wrote you the apology letter,
which healed you from the bite of the guard
dog. Would you like to be able to visit
it all the time? Or would you rather stare
at the cold, closed high wall that I usually
show you?
The choice is yours.
- How should I ask her? -

Help! He's out of control!
The teenager's world of tension

A word of encouragement:

While it is certainly best for a younger child to learn anger management skills that include anticipating or warding off situations that make life more difficult and confusing, it should not be assumed that a teenager's aggressive behavior is a hopeless cause. There are reasons, however, why it becomes more difficult to help a teenager:

1. Hormonal changes are occurring, so brain chemistry is also changing. Medications that worked well may no longer be effective. An altered metabolism creates new challenges, new behaviors and much stronger emotions. Teenaged bodies experience enormous change, but teenagers with neurological or physical challenges are very likely not following the "normal" track. This is confusing for you, them, and often their doctors.

2. Lack of organization or just a disregard for tidiness may present a significant problem at this age. If messiness is a concern, the result may be more than just a sloppy bedroom; it may also cause over-stimulation. In short...their own stuff may be driving them crazy!

3. Privacy may be a big issue. If so, it is REALLY a problem now, because teenagers don't want anyone messing with their stuff! They also may not be as willing to share information with you...even good information!

4. There are more physical, social and scholastic opportunities, but desires for independence may not match realistic skill levels. Teenagers have a tendency to take on more than they are capable of doing. They may not be mature enough or have the stamina to handle a long list of responsibilities.

5. Acceptance from peers is important, but may sometimes be unattainable when skills are not similar. Teenagers, like most of us, want acceptance from others, but other kids' abilities may exceed those of a teen with special challenges. There is a need to set one's own standards, expectations and activities and learn to appreciate them.

6. There is increasing awareness that they don't fit into the social world their peers enjoy. Challenged teenagers may also begin to realize that the people they enjoy being with are not actually "peers." This makes them much less likely to fit into the "normal" social settings at school. They might become the target for teasing if they spend free time with teachers and older adults or choose younger children as friends.

7. Teens sometimes just like a good fight or debating challenge. It is difficult for parents to know when a teen is just trying out a new idea, asking for attention or challenging authority.

8. Rage may also look or feel like hopelessness. It is easier to give up hope than continue fighting to be understood, but the giving up may lead to rage. Many of those with autism or other neurological differences do not have the ability to have a range of feelings, so they may not be aware they are experiencing anger until it is upon them...and often only after they have committed an act.

By the time Kate became a teenager, her anger management skills were pretty well developed, so rage was not an issue, but there were still a few behaviors we found bewildering:

1. Her changing metabolism and shifting hormones created new problems and new behaviors.

2. Her language skills were greater, but it became increasingly more difficult to gauge her comprehension. Because of her increased independence, the stakes for clear communication became higher.

3. Our expectations for her were sometimes out of sync with her ability to perform skills, i.e. self-care.

4. Other kids were doing things that she wasn't doing. We knew it was difficult for Kate to develop her own set of standards, expectations and activities.

Children who haven't learned healthy and effective skills for handling frustration enter adolescence and early adulthood utilizing poor anger management methods. Their responses have become mastered and are applied instinctively. It becomes increasingly more difficult for them to learn new responses. In teens that have not learned to channel anger appropriately you may see the following behaviors:

1. Acts of aggression may begin. Teens can be physically big enough to inflict serious damage on themselves, other people or property. Teens are at greater risk because the public and law enforcement officers are much less "forgiving" of aggressive acts at this age.

33

2. Teens may tease and cast insults on siblings or younger children.

3. Unhappy teens often don't go anywhere. They have few hobbies, and few (if any) friends.

4. Issues of privacy become conflicting and confusing. Many teens relish their privacy but are not clear about what is considered a private issue. Those teens with special challenges may not seem to value privacy at all. This creates a potential for major battles. If privacy and independence are large issues, they may not be willing to let you assist them.

5. They have unrealistic expectations. Teens see what others do and want what others have. Rather than forming their own set of standards, teens often assume they can be like other people they admire. Teens may not have the necessary skills to handle situations they believe "everyone else" is handling; yet they are embarrassed to admit their inexperience or choose to ignore advice. Their ignorance can often lead to making poor choices.

6. Teens desperately want control, so they create situations where you will likely lose yours!

7. Teens have more access to drugs, alcohol, fast cars, etc. Truly depressed teens may seek avoidance of pain in scary ways.

Inciting to riot

Stressors make life difficult for many of our kids who come in "other flavors." Actually, all kids have most of those stressors, but not all kids will experience frustration to the same degree. We need to realize that many things contribute to our feelings and our ability to cope with a situation or emotion. How hungry or tired we feel may determine how well we deal with other stressors in our day. Someone explained to me that an over-stimulated or stressed mind is like a surge to an electrical system. The overload may make the lights in your house get very bright for just a second, but then the bulb will burn out, causing a complete shutdown or fire.

We all experience unfounded fears, but people with have neurological differences have much more difficulty getting and assimilating information, so they experience fear to a greater degree. Once autistic people realize they are not always getting the proper messages from faces and language, they become even more anxious. They know they can't trust what they perceive and this disability makes them feel apprehensive in settings where they must function as though they have no special challenges.

Here's a checklist that can help determine why your child might be struggling. Remember, many of these issues may be occurring at the same time. As you use this list, pay close attention to your child, gather clues and plan strategies.

1. Delayed fine motor skills leading to school stresses and awkward social skills

2. Erratic brain chemistry

3. Sleeplessness

4. Food allergies or change in diet

5. Excessive hunger (a very frequent occurrence!)

6. Change in routine/schedule, people, medication or environment

7. Lack of control over body and environment

8. Feelings of loss or inability to control everyday situations - such as riding a bus, or navigating through a crowded hallway

9. Unrealistic expectations regarding body image

10. Unrealistic expectations regarding performance in games, athletic events, school conquests

11. Unclear expectations and rules from parents, teachers, peers

12. Fear of failure

13. Feeling overwhelmed and anxious when confronting a large task or a new activity (even one the teen chooses for himself!)

14. Being expected to do or be something that is not mentally or physically possible

15. Fear of success (bringing unwanted attention) and/or fear of next step expected

16. Being noticed or highlighted for ANY reason

17. Excessive stimulation

18. Sensory defensiveness, in which there is an inappropriate reaction to extremes of external stimuli

19. Attempt to self-limit perseveration *(stimming) or *tics

20. Desire for more freedom, yet without the self-control to handle the freedom responsibly

21. Teasing/bullying

22. Being abused by someone else or abuse to self

Does it solve the problem?

If you're like I am, you may have a tendency to cut to the chase in times of severe desperation and not get all the background information you need to adequately solve a problem. In that light, I implore you to read the earlier section of the book before diving into this section of proposed solutions. It is imperative to understand the motivations or causes for a behavior in order to successfully change that behavior. Afterwards you'll be better equipped to know which of the solutions, or tips, provided in this book will work with your child. Your own insights will help you develop unique solutions and strategies. The ultimate goal of the book is not to tell you how to manage your lives, but rather to encourage you to discover your own paths.

Defining criteria for effective methods of anger managment

A word about strategies:

In our house we use basic criteria to decide if a skill is a "good" one.

1. Does it hurt you?
2. Does it hurt anyone else?
3. Do you feel better after having used the strategy?
4. Is it effective? Does it solve the problem?

Some strategies do not completely solve the problem, but are effective for allowing you to let off some steam. Venting may be necessary to pave the way for more rational thought, so it is a worthwhile process. In our house, if we want to peacefully settle the problem, the process ultimately involves honest conversation.

Examples of appropriate and inappropriate ways to vent anger for our daughter include going to her room and making noise, hitting and throwing pillows in her room or playing the piano LOUDLY (as long as she is not damaging the instrument in any way). She finally knows that talking about her problem works best! As an adult, she is willing to be forthcoming about her perceptions and feelings. I haven't seen Kate act physically aggressive in about a decade. She realizes that honest communication is really the only thing that uncovers a true solution. Kate is free to say, "I hate it when..." She needs the freedom to express her anger verbally, but without being venomous to the other person. She has to be willing to discuss the issue, not just the person's undesired qualities. I won't punish her for her infrequent, whispered profanities; she's heard her father and me voice a few expletives in times of frustration. I think that quietly whispered, well-chosen words are sometimes the most effective way to diffuse some anger, but we should make every effort not to say them to the person, just ABOUT an issue. When I recollect some of the negative behaviors Kate has left behind, I almost applaud when I hear her say, "!*#!" under her breath when she spills something. That's much better than throwing orange slush or having a loud temper tantrum. It gives an immediate release for small incidents, or in the event of a more significant problem, may relieve a pent-up feeling and make discussion a bit calmer and more successful.

One of the earliest steps toward anger management is helping children recognize when they are getting angry. It would be so much better if they could feel it coming on...so that their anger was more (as my friend, Dave Spicer says) like a faucet, rather than an on-off switch. Teaching them to become aware of their own precipitators and the situations or issues they find frustrating is very important. Sometimes the precipitators are particular people or various topics of discussion. Children might be triggered into a state of frenzy by sound, lights or crowds, etc. Knowing when to be aware of these possible DANGER zones will help them work through or even avoid a precarious situation. Careful attention on both our parts helped Kate practice calming down and thinking through her actions, before she was out of control and reacting to extreme frustrations.

I don't think kids intend to get into trouble. Their inappropriate behavior to a given situation is just a reaction to stress. Most often, they get into trouble due to their own ignorance or inability to use skills that would effect a positive change. To put it simply, they don't know what else to do; they react impulsively with only limited tools at their disposal. The tools they use may not be successful in solving the problem at hand, but rather make the entire situation worse. People become accustomed to acting in predetermined ways in certain situations. They don't stop to think first. If, instead, they instinctively practice problem-solving skills that are successful, they are less likely to experience conflict. What worked with Kate was to give her some new options, which I describe in the next sections. Similar to breaking a bad habit, a new behavior must be learned and reinforced before it can insert itself without a parent's intervention.

Hitting, biting, kicking and such

Hitting seems to be one of the earliest acts of aggression that small children commit. The first and most important step for us was to remove Kate's targets for their own protection. We couldn't allow other children to be harmed by Kate. The second step, after we demonstrated examples of appropriate play to her, was to reintroduce play in a very supervised way: Kate would only play with one other child at first. We preferred choosing a playmate for Kate that was pretty "tough" and more occupied with toys or objects than with other children. That seemed to divert both kids. When she was older we helped her become aware of frustrating situations and intervened on the spot with the appropriate language she could use when angry or wanting attention. In the case of anger management we might say, "It's okay to be angry, it's not okay to hit, bite or kick. You are a big girl. When you are angry you have words. They work much better. They help fix it. Hitting just makes it worse. Now Kate, what do you do when you are angry?" I had to repeat these phrases to Kate so many times I sounded like a broken record, but she finally got it. She learned to reply, "Talk about it." I'd ask the question and get her to repeat the answer at least five times. When she saw I was willing to really listen to her problems or feelings, the physical aggression greatly diminished.

Since Kate is an *Aspie, I often had to help her guess how she was feeling. She didn't yet have the words to describe her feelings. So I tried to help her learn those particular vocabulary words and the feelings that corresponded to them. At first we used very simple words, then gradually helped her extend her thoughts and sentences. She also began to realize that she received more positive attention for NOT hitting. I tried to catch her just before she was ready to strike, then would call loudly, "Kate!" When I had her attention I would quickly ask, "What do we do when we're angry?" Her response had to be practiced repeatedly until it became instinctive. This strategy worked pretty well for us. We still gave her appropriate physical activities she could do when she was angry such as running or hitting a pillow.

42

Obviously these alternatives didn't solve the problem but did get rid of the physical stress.

One friend said she finally explained to her adolescent son that what he was doing (violently striking others with his hands and feet) was called assault and battery, and if the aggressive acts continued into adulthood he would wind up in jail. My friend believed her son knew the difference between right and wrong, but he would react without any forethought when he was angry or felt he had been treated unjustly. Apparently that piece of information helped him find new ways of expressing his need for justice.

Currently, Kate's anger management skills are quite developed. She does a few other things I'm not crazy about; none are acts of anger and most of them involve MY clothes and MY make-up, but I no longer worry about her being jailed for assault. MK

Tantrums

We all have witnessed tantrums, and we all have opinions about the person experiencing the tantrum as well as the person whom we think should be controlling it! Let's examine them a little more carefully (than we generally do when witnessing one in the aisle at the corner grocery store).

There are differing degrees and causes of tantrums or meltdowns. In order to best help the child, the cause of the tantrum needs to be determined. Some children will need medication, and others will need behavior modification. Still others will just require cool-down techniques. All will need training to recognize when a tantrum is approaching.

I think there are two kinds of tantrums:

1. The tantrum of manipulation occurs when children think they can win something by embarrassing you or wearing you down. Ignore this if possible! Just make sure the child is as safe as you would were your child having a seizure. When a calmer period has returned, you can teach your child more effective and positive ways of gaining attention or control.

2. The second type of tantrum results from being tired, frustrated, confused or over-stimulated. Generally, letting kids rant on for a while will decrease their anger; like a storm, it will eventually blow itself out. Do beware, however, that kids with challenges often don't have the ability to de-escalate, so their anger may become greater.

When recalling my own tantrums as a child, I realized they actually had NOTHING to do with anyone else's behavior or reaction. I simply didn't know any other way to release my frustration or express exhaustion from over-stimulation. My natural inclination was to lie on the floor or in the backseat of the car kicking and screaming. (Sorry, Mother!) When I learned other methods of dealing with my feelings, I stopped having them. Thank goodness my mother didn't feel responsible for my behavior; nor did she punish, ridicule, or react angrily to my tantrums. She just continued to teach good examples for more effective stress relieving behaviors. (By the way, I behave relatively well now ;-) MK

As parents, we must remember that our child's behavior usually has nothing to do with us. We can be pretty egocentric. We assume our child's feelings are in direct response to our parenting. I tried to help Kate learn effective options for expressing her feelings, just as I had to learn other ways of channeling my own anger.

I am of the opinion that you handle both types of tantrums the same way as long as the tantrum is in action. Once the tantrum is over, the skills a parent teaches to help avoid further outbursts will be different. Regardless of the new skills to be learned, all must be taught in a teachable moment. You're wasting your time if you try to teach during the height of crisis, highly emotional times or during a rush for time. Privacy, a calm environment and a non-judgmental attitude are needed to make your teaching time meaningful and useable. Also, remember that you'll need to re-teach and remind. It takes awhile to establish new habits. During times of crisis, people typically react on impulse only, so be patient for change to occur. There is a pretty steep learning curve.

It is critical that a child (or adult) learns that resorting to a loud, manipulative tantrum is ineffective. While what they desire may be legitimate, it's imperative they learn that a tantrum won't work in their favor and, in fact, makes them less persuasive in their demands. Specific suggestions for ways to change behavior need to be clearly stated without bias and practiced during periods of calm. (*Role-play works well in this instance.) If allowed to continue for an extended period of time, a manipulative tantrum can escalate into an uncontrolled *meltdown, one the child can no longer stop even if they have the desire to do so.

In either type, the first concern must be safety: for the person having the tantrum, for yourself, for others and for property. Don't be afraid to get help from neighbors, store security staff, the police or medical personnel. Safety takes precedence. Embarrassment really isn't the first concern! The public will follow your lead. If you are acting in a focused and controlled manner, any bystanders will more likely be supportive rather than judgmental or rude. Make it clear to your child that there are certain basic and firm guidelines to follow when out in public:

1. Explain clearly that tantrums are simply not allowed.

2. Limit the amount of time you and your child are out of the home.

3. Help your child win time outside the home by demonstrating good behavior inside the home. Kate would lose opportunities anytime her behavior was out of control in public, so my husband and I used this disciplinary action as part of a behavior modification program. We began with managing simple behaviors, in limited situations, before we branched out. Kate didn't perceive these imposed limitations

46

as punishment. She understood the benefit of practicing her skills with family members at home first. Gradually she was ready to attempt bigger and more enduring challenges in different environments. Eventually, Kate's newly learned behaviors entitled her to interactions with people other than family members.

As the observer of a tantrum, there are a few techniques you can use to manage the situation and protect yourself more confidently. These strategies may even defuse a tantrum before it occurs. A professional anger management instructor who deals with people who experience tantrums shared some general tips with me. According to him, introduction of these techniques has significantly decreased the frequency of tantrum behaviors in his classes.

1. Either stay out of arms/legs reach or stay very close. If you remain close, stay behind the child. The easiest way to turn a person around is by pushing forward with a cupped and open hand above his elbow. The body turns pretty easily. Then reach under the other arm and grasp his wrist. With the hand that is at the elbow, keep it there or slide it to the inside of the arm. You find yourself behind the person, holding onto to one arm—and staying close. You can soothe and talk calmly to the person—so it isn't a "fight." You are "bear-hugging" the person until they calm themselves down.

2. If the person is on the floor kicking, keep objects out of the way and use pillows when approaching the person to prevent being kicked. You may want to just let them kick away rather than risk getting hurt by intervening.

47

Early tantrum management

When a person becomes skilled enough to recognize the early symptoms of a tantrum, follow the strategies listed below:

1. Help him see the situation in another light, one that will make him laugh. Laughter provides the same physical release as a tantrum.

2. Make available things that would be calming, i.e. lower lights and/or sound, set a cool drink near the child, change environment (fewer people, soothing music or sound).

3. Provide uninterrupted time for behavior to cool down.

4. Try different methods that give clear direction about the stages building up to a tantrum. One mother I know said that her son responds well when she uses a "3-count" strategy. "For example, when our son is angry and venting with a tantrum, and it's gone on for a while and is becoming a ritual rather than a real vent, we use the three count as a focus: 'Larry, we're going to count to three now. One, take a deep breath and let it out slowly (it takes time to get past "one" sometimes). Two, take another deep breath and unclench your body. Three, let out your breath and calm out.' This works unless he's really upset, which means there's something else going on that he can't access immediately. In this case, we wait until the episode has passed and then talk it out."

48

5. Consider medical help for managing uncontrollable behavior. Some tantrums are reactions to body chemistry changes and may require medical intervention. Several medications used for seizure disorders can also be used successfully to treat behavior disorders.

6. Some incidents that appear to be temper tantrums may be chemically based physiologic reactions. When Kate was four-years-old, her doctor prescribed a new medication that incidentally caused uncontrollable aggression. I spent many hours that day holding her firmly in my lap, my arms wrapped tightly around all four of her limbs, to keep her from hurting herself or me. It was clearly an adverse reaction from the new drug and just had to be waited out. Be advised that new medications must be closely monitored.

7. Seek ways to teach the child about tantrums and how others perceive him when he expresses his feelings in this inappropriate way. You might call his attention to another person you see in public who is out of control. If you encounter someone who's really lost it, like a younger kid in a toy store, it might be helpful to gently point out that that's how *he* looks when he has a tantrum.

There are times, however, when a small tantrum is probably no worse than voicing profanity. Under the right circumstances, and as long as you don't hurt yourself, other people or property, throwing a tantrum might actually be an acceptable tension reliever. When you consider some of the more dangerous stress relievers (alcohol, drugs and abuse) a bit of a tantrum in the privacy of your closet might even be considered a little healthy!

*Non-physical meltdowns

A person who is unable to function in a positive way is experiencing a non-physical meltdown. The meltdown is similar to the tantrum that is not for "show" or meant to manipulate. The person does not display physical aggression but may seem agitated, out of touch with his surroundings or unable to focus on a subject or conversation. Someone experiencing a non-physical meltdown needs a quiet place where he can calm down after too much stimulation, change or overwhelming circumstance.

In these situations a person may be soothed by some simple methods. A parent or friend can just call his name, quietly and repeatedly. If the person is not sensory defensive, softly rubbing his shoulders could do the trick. With a soft voice you can say, "I can see that you really want me to understand what's going on. It's okay if you do things at your own pace. Everyone needs to relax." Acknowledging his feelings as legitimate is often the most assuring thing you can do. Reflecting on his feelings and helping him problem-solve is effective once he has become calm. Sometimes the person just needs time to be alone, in a quiet setting.

*School Issues

Many parents and students experience intense anger when facing complex situations that occur at school. Proper planning and classroom placement have a lot to do with handling school anger. There are many good books about handling behaviors in the educational setting, therefore, I will not deal at length with school issues. I will, however, give just a few brief comments about common situations that create stress for students and suggest ways you might help your child reduce the experience of intense anger while at school.

1. If your child is having difficulty managing assignments, you could ask the teacher to write the assignment on the board and let him copy it. This strategy would benefit the entire class.

2. If possible, consider your child's ideas when planning classroom goals and expectations. He is more likely to follow through if he understands the general goals and contributes to the specific items that meet his individual needs.

3. If classroom noise disturbs him, and he can't concentrate, suggest the use of a study *carrell. This is a partition a student can erect on his desk to provide a "quiet zone." Another option is to provide a desk that faces a back wall in the classroom so he will be less distracted. He can sit with the class for the lecture, then go to his private area to work. He probably won't be the only one to use it. Other non-traditional kids have this same problem.

4. The attitude that is expected in the classroom is set and modeled by the teacher, so help your child develop a rapport with him or her. This will help the teacher and student have positive feelings and respect for each other. A teacher who respects every student is easily identified. Insist on respect for yourself and for your children. When we spend time with those who don't respect us, eventually we don't respect ourselves. What inevitably follow are anger, depression, and hostility.

At the suggestion of a trusted friend and principal, we took Kate out of the overwhelming public school system at the beginning of her first grade year and provided her with a much calmer homeschool setting. We attempted to put Kate in the public school system on three occasions during her grade school years. Each time her behavior, academic skills and self-esteem suffered, so we decided to homeschool her. We also received lots of assistance from some dedicated tutors and community resources. Homeschooling allowed Kate to practice life skills and social behavior in a real way, in actual settings where her new skills were necessary.

During her homeschooling years, we had the opportunity to truly understand Kate's strengths and weaknesses. We selected the most beneficial mentors for her to model, rather than the most academically outstanding students in the classroom. Kate needed to see a wide variety of behaviors, not just academic achievement. Finding strong role models is imperative for learning and practicing behavioral management skills.

Much to our surprise, advancing into the college setting proved to be very easy. There were few social cliques; the teachers in one department were not concerned with a student's level of achievement in another. Schedules were more flexible and could be coordinated to suit Kate's best cognitive thinking times. Best of all, Kate could control the amount of stress she imposed on herself; she could take one course only or five at a time.

*Behavior Modification

Behavior modification helps establish new patterns and shows that rewards can be more valuable than just a tangible treat or snack. Children and adults use this method consciously and unconsciously. Modification is very effective when a behavior that requires change is replaced with an alternate behavior that insures a more positive outcome. People respond well when a substitute behavior that still fulfills a need or desire is provided, rather than telling them to just stop the inappropriate action. Behaviors to be changed in anger management may involve curbing or stopping destructive behaviors. As an example, a child can earn tickets each hour for meeting certain criteria such as no verbal abuse, no violence or no destructive behavior. The tickets are given a value, perhaps ten cents. When the child has earned sufficient tickets (as well as praise for trying to act appropriately), he can redeem them for a reward.

Many types of behavior modification have been used. They provide a non-judgmental, easily tracked and distinguishable cause/effect response that many find helpful. Consistent behavior always produces consistent results. All of us are creatures of habit, but those with neurological challenges often find changing a habit more difficult. Because this method clearly rewards a specific behavior in a consistent way, this method of learning is quite successful. The key to success is in the consistency provided by the parent or person monitoring the behavior and providing the reward.

Behavior modification may be easily established with a "parent-child contract." To work well, the child has to agree that the chosen modification is a worthwhile goal. Simply put, both you and the kid want the behavior altered. Agree on a reward; it should be something tangible, (coins, television time, game with

53

Dad, etc.) Gold stars on a chart are okay, but not at first. The idea is to give the kid an immediate reward for replacing the undesired behavior with a more desirable one. For example, if your kid typically bangs his head on the wall whenever he gets angry, you first reward him for being angry but *not banging* his head on the wall. There should be no penalty for not meeting the goal. I don't make my daughter return her rewards if she fails; I just don't reinforce the inappropriate behaviors. You can gradually work up to delayed gratification where a gold star is earned for each success and stars are accumulated until the reward is earned. It is important that the child understands what the gold stars represent and gets recognition for his efforts.

When Kate was a young adolescent we had great success with behavior modification. We finally understood the need to communicate specific expectations with her. Generalities were lost on Kate. Behavior modification rewards increased Kate's willingness to try new behaviors repeatedly. She felt comfortable with our supervision because she received an instant reaction and knew precisely if she had behaved appropriately.

Behavior modifications change periodically, and so must the rewards. Changes are dependent on the age of the child and what is important to him. I don't believe you should reward with food, and Kate needed something else that was tangible. We used nickels when Kate was nine because she needed to be working on money skills. Using money also provided an example of money earned for behavior (since most jobs are definitely linked to money and successful work practices). At first she needed to collect the nickel reward immediately. We gradually could award the total coins earned in a day. Once Kate began to experience the intrinsic reward earned from positive feedback, she even forgot to ask for the nickel!

54

I have one last word about behavior modification. The person whose behavior is undergoing the program must have the physical ability to make the change. If body chemistry or too small a bladder is the problem, this program will not only fail but will create much stress for both the child and the parent. Be sure the desired behavior is possible and controllable by the child.

Decision-making

Another major issue Kate had when she was about seven years old involved her fear of decision-making. It took a while for her dad and me to figure out what was causing her intense anger when she was asked to make a decision. We thought she was just "out of sorts." Gradually we realized that she was unhappy with *anything* she chose. Our quest to let Kate gain independence threw her into a major control crisis. Apparently, she felt she could not trust herself to make the right decision. I think it was a push-pull thing with power. "I do want control of some things in my life, but what if I do the wrong thing?!" She wanted control, but the control scared her. I thought it was time that she made some of her own decisions and had assumed she would be pleased with that option. Unfortunately, I didn't realize she felt inadequate to do so. We worked through a series of steps to help her become confident and happy with her choices.

Kate was already a successful decision maker, but she needed to be reminded. By highlighting all the successes she met each day from making choices, she gradually became aware of her own capability. During the day, I would casually point out that she had made a decision and how well it worked out. "Oh, you made the decision to watch that show! You enjoy it, don't you! Good Choice!" Another time I might say, "You've chosen to wear your pink socks today. They are beautiful! Good choice!"

55

She was totally unaware that her day was filled with choices. I didn't point out that by deciding to watch one show, she was missing another, nor the fact that she chose pink socks everyday! There was no good reason to ask for trouble. Instead, I consistently reinforced her successes and her confidence grew, but the process still involved small steps.

The second step is hard for many people. Kate began to realize that when you say, "Yes" to something you are saying, "No" to something else. We all have to learn that when we make a choice to enter through one door, we are in effect closing others. In Kate's process, we eventually concluded that what my husband and I perceived as an opportunity, Kate viewed as a loss. We would go to get yogurt, and she would FINALLY say she wanted chocolate. However, as soon as I ordered the chocolate, she would become intensely angry and yell that, in fact, she wanted vanilla. It eventually occurred to me how to handle this: I told her that this decision was only for THIS time. I explained that we would be coming again, and next time she could order vanilla. We helped her understand that many choices are made for short-term gains only, and new options arise daily. This information had a very calming effect for Kate.

The next step involved Kate's recognition that there may be more than one "right" decision. To prevent Kate from feeling overwhelmed with too many choices, we limited her selection. We set up instances where she would make an identical choice several times. In one case, we went to a favorite hamburger place, and she would choose first between only two flavors of ice cream...chocolate or vanilla. We did that several times until Kate could finally accept her choice willingly, (she would scream that's NOT what she wanted, or refuse to eat it, or throw it at you!) Then we went to a yogurt place and let her choose from among three flavors. I picked what her choices could be; I chose vanilla, chocolate and then some kind that I knew she would hate, so she was actually left with choosing between two kinds. Then, I'd let her choose from among three flavors she did like: chocolate, vanilla and strawberry. The next time I'd give her four choices, with three she liked and one she hated, etc. I kept using this sequential pattern until decisions were MUCH easier, (and we all weighed a bit more!)

When she finally understood that there could be more than one "right" decision, she settled down. We also made sure she understood that she would get another opportunity at another time to make a different choice. "Not today" did not mean "never."

Finally Kate understood that most decisions didn't involve a right or wrong answer. Choices and decisions weren't generally good or bad, just different. That information was enlightening to her and greatly improved her ability to make decisions. It meant that sometimes you couldn't miss. Anything you decided in certain circumstances was a great decision. It was a big confidence builder.

My editor asked me if choosing yogurt as Kate's incentive conflicted with my dislike of using food as a reward...well, yes, but we needed to create a clearly defined situation that Kate would be interested in. In the end, Kate had to modify her behavior in order to succeed at decision-making. Without an appealing incentive, Kate would never have been so motivated. MK

Speech and language skills

As a young adult, Kate understands that she must use language, even if all she says is, "I'm mad!" That kind of outburst at least gives us a starting place for discussion. However, when she was seven and eight, we had to teach her to talk through her anger by giving her specific language to use. It was like writing a script for her to practice. Now she can alter the script, but she still knows the "language" for expressing anger: "I'm mad when... I thought you said... Next time...Let's negotiate... Let's take turns... It hurts me when...I'm embarrassed when... It scares me when..." etc.

It was also important to help her recognize facial expressions of other people. We spent a lot of time watching television and discussing how facial expressions gave clues to the story. We listened to the way people spoke to one another and analyzed how they reacted to anger. We made masks that would show various expressions. Rather than letting Kate strike out aggressively, we showed Kate how to use those masks to help her speak about her feelings. We gave Kate extra practice with the masks during calmer moments, too. We incorporated role-play techniques so Kate could pretend she was feeling what a particular mask showed. She could talk about the emotion displayed on the mask; yet remain detached from the emotion herself. She could also explore what choices "the mask" could make if it was feeling sad, nervous, bored, or mad. This kind of play broadened her expressive vocabulary and increased her awareness of the many types of emotions people can have.

Please Match!

Inside feeling not matching outside behavior.

Don't assume that what you see is what he feels.

My insides feel: ## My outsides show:

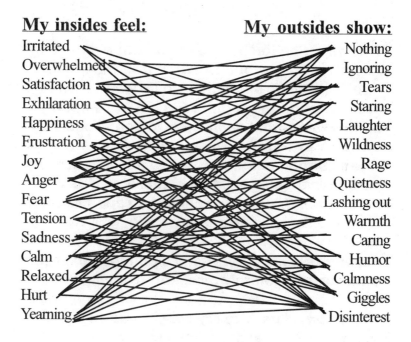

My insides feel:	My outsides show:
Irritated	Nothing
Overwhelmed	Ignoring
Satisfaction	Tears
Exhilaration	Staring
Happiness	Laughter
Frustration	Wildness
Joy	Rage
Anger	Quietness
Fear	Lashing out
Tension	Warmth
Sadness	Caring
Calm	Humor
Relaxed	Calmness
Hurt	Giggles
Yearning	Disinterest

Get the picture?

Difficulty controlling, monitoring or understanding emotions of self and others.

by Martha Kate Downey

copyright 1999 *TAP DANCING in the night*

Thoughts on Feelings

"My emotions are like a light switch - either off or on. I wish they were more adjustable like water coming from a faucet." (Adult with AS)

"This might be too obvious to mention, but I think that part of our problem with not APPEARING to be empathetic might have to do with trying to mask or suppress a great EXCESS of empathy - almost to a fault. I really have to consciously try to suppress over-reactions to other's strong emotions. The result is frequently a deadpan reaction, that is interpreted as not caring, even though I am being torn apart inside."- Brett (Adult with AS)

"Feelings sneak up on you...I didn't recognize fear until I was absolutely terrified!" (Adult with AS)

"funny, I used to cry when I was angry. Now I get angry when I want to cry - quite sure this is no improvement." - Eric (age 27 with AS)

60

Remember that what you say may not be understood, or understood as you intended.

Many people with neurological challenges, especially those having autistic traits, can repeat what you say, but have little or no comprehension of the words they heard or repeated. We had some very difficult months until I figured this out. Kate had trouble understanding opposites, so she used them inappropriately. When traveling in the car I would ask if she were too cold. Her response would be, "Yes," and I would turn on the heater. Then she would say in a very frustrated voice, "I told you it was too cold!" What she meant was that she was too hot already. When we taught ourselves to use sign language, a whole new world opened up. If I asked the same question in sign language, Kate's answer accurately reflected her feelings. Hot is hot and cold is cold. In is in and out is out. What a deal for us all! The tactile and visual parts of her brain understood language much better than the hearing part of her brain.

You might try simple signs for yes/no, hot/cold, on top/below, older/younger, etc. You may not experience this condition of autism, but we did. The language deficit affected Kate's decision-making ability as well. No wonder she was frustrated; she couldn't trust herself to verbalize what she really meant. No wonder she was afraid of decisions…they turned out wrong too often.

Breathing techniques

There is a direct connection between breathing patterns and body tension. Any woman who has experienced natural childbirth will agree that when appropriate breathing techniques are used, the pain of labor is reduced. When stress and frustration overwhelm a child, these same techniques may be used to achieve a positive, purposeful effect as well. An example is to exhale slowly between pursed lips. Try it; you'll feel your spine relax.

Controlled breathing techniques give a child the chance to get his words organized enough to talk about his growing anxiety rather than striking out in a physical way. Breathing is a physical occupation, and thus gives him something to DO with his anxiety. Bystanders also realize that the disturbed person is making a conscious effort to control his anger and respond in a way that is not hurtful, but rather productive, toward solving the problem. Most of us will go the extra mile for someone if we know he is trying to work on a problem. We feel relieved and heartened that he is taking responsibility for his physical reactions to stress.

A time of intense anger is NOT the time to teach new techniques. Teach when the person is calm and receptive toward making new choices about his behavior. A quick way to teach pattern breathing is to count as you breath in and out. Have the child focus and breathe along with you, according to your pattern. Then tell him to become aware of how many counts it takes for him to inhale and exhale comfortably. "In, 2, 3...Out, 2, 3" is a fairly reliable count. Teach him that when he becomes angry, his pattern changes. The idea is to interrupt the cycle of frustration early. When he begins to feel angry, prompt the child to consciously count his breaths. Ultimately, this will force his metabolism back into a more normal rhythm. This technique has three main components: by becoming aware of an increase in respiration, a child can more easily recognize the onset of anxiety; a change in the pattern signifies approaching anger; and awareness of the physical change alerts the child to use his new breathing techniques to control his body and avoid a tantrum.

Right or Wrong

Black must be black and white must be white.
They give me straight answers, don't muddy my sight.
Gray tells me nothing! It chases away
the clarity needed to get through a day.

Don't change the rules on me, confuse and ignore.
My mode of rigidity comforts me more.
Let me keep my black safety. Let me focus on white,
'cause the gray that you bring causes terrible

con fu s ion!

By Martha Kate Downey
copyright 1999 *TAP DANCING in the night*

Perfectionism

Our children with neurological differences frequently have problems with perfectionism. To them, everything is either all correct or all wrong. The biggest problem is that this attitude rules out any variance for human error and diminishes self-esteem. For many of our special kids, earning 95% on a paper is as "bad" as getting a 65%. If their work is not all right, then it must be all wrong! The task of developing realistic expectations is a tough one. Everyone (myself included!) deals with this issue throughout life, but because our kiddos have problems understanding society and its expectations, they have difficulties establishing reasonable levels of achievement for themselves. I found a way to help Kate identify levels of achievement and separate her self-esteem and our love for her from the numbers given on a paper.

I asked Kate, "If you make 100% on a paper do you think you are a good person?" Then I asked, "Do Daddy and I love you when you make 100% on a paper?" She answered both questions affirmatively. I went on to ask if she were a good person and if Daddy and I would love her if she made a 99%. She said, "Yes," very slowly and carefully, watching my face for signals to see if she had gotten the "right" answer. I told her, "I agree, you are a good person and we will always love you." I went on to ask if she were still a good person if she made a 98%. I asked if we would still love her if she made a 98%. You can guess by now where I was going with this, although I continued this method of questioning for several more minutes. Eventually Kate realized that her family loved and valued her regardless of numbers on a paper. She even spent several minutes making repetitious statements about her self-worth. She came to realize that the numbers only indicated how prepared she was for the particular classroom assignment and had no relationship to our love for her or how she should value herself as a person.

I took this lesson one step further. Since Kate had complained that her school paper was terrible, I suggested that we review it together. Without warning I began to read aloud questions that she had already answered correctly. In a way I was teasing Kate, and she recognized it quickly enough. *Why was her paper so terrible if she got so many right answers?* It's true that teasing can be cruel, but when you use a sense of humor it can honor or affirm a positive trait about someone. My good-natured teasing boosted Kate's pride and helped her realize that all a test shows are those areas where she still has opportunity for growth.

Until you address the basic reason for the anger, you will not be solving the problem, just attaching a band-aid to cover it up. Perfectionism has to do with self-worth. Realizing that achievement is measured with levels or standards is valuable to Kate, but doesn't change the value she places on herself.

Choose the good

I have worked and worked to teach my children to "CHOOSE THE GOOD." To us that means choosing good friends, books, movies, etc. Kate took the concept even further. One summer she was acting as an aide in a computer classroom where a student addressed her in a condescending manner. According to Kate, the student told her he didn't have to listen to her, "You're just a retard." Kate said another student sitting nearby heard the comment and remarked, "You'd better listen to her. She knows more about computers than you ever will." Kate's summation of the interaction was, "Wasn't that a nice thing for him to say!" She had let the negative statement go right on by and instead chose to accept the compliment as the highlight of the encounter. That's what I mean about choosing the good. Choose the good in your life and let the rest go!

When we "choose the good" we can choose to not let comments from others affect us to a great extent, especially if the comment is confusing. I suggest that we trust our history with a person and let the positive encounters override any one single comment or behavior. If, in the past, someone has been kind to you, honor that knowledge and overlook a piece of gossip that *only might* have been said maliciously. When we spend our time looking for the good in our lives, we are much more likely to live in a positive frame of mind.

> *"It's all a matter of choice. If someone has hurt my feelings or told a joke I don't catch (which is very often), I choose not to put my emotions into a tailspin. I choose to let it go with a shrug. I choose to think that most people are not out there gunning for me"*
> *MK.*

Formulating strategies

Here are a few more suggestions to consider as you form strategies for anger management:

1. Be aware that to actually solve a problem you must discover its underlying cause. As in the example of perfectionism, it was not enough to tell Kate that making a 95% on a test was a very good score. She had more going on in her mind than just numbers on a paper. She was dealing with two basic issues: bad versus good; and fear that she was not worth 100% to us or to herself. It was crucially important to assure Kate of her worth before tackling anything else. Take Sister Margaret's advice very seriously as you study your child and work toward developing his anger management skills. You don't want the child to just stop having tantrums; you want him to actually have better skills to manage daily frustrations. Watch out for quick fixes that only cover up underlying needs for healing and growing.

2. Identify someone who can provide honest feedback about people, emotions, situations, etc. Because our children often have difficulty with perceptual skills, they may be relying on false information when making decisions and value judgments. This trusted person should help verify information that might frighten or anger your child, especially before heavy rage sets in.

   I know this method works. I have a friend who is an athlete on our Special Olympics team. She has learned to pull me aside during a practice for a quick discussion when she is confused about something. She trusts me and uses me as a sounding board to help her make the appropriate responses that by-pass many hostile feelings. She was 44-years-old when she began using this strategy, and consequently, she is slowly changing her own thought and reaction patterns. I think this idea works even better if you can find someone to be a sounding board/problem-solver before your child reaches maturity. Actually, most of us do this unconsciously because we think about something before reacting. However, a child with neurological difficulties has to overcome an additional step: learning *what* to think about. Until the circumstance or feeling is identified, an autistic or Aspie kid can't even move on to *thinking* about it, let alone *reacting* to it. The helpful mentor gives the child a clue about what's really going on in a particular situation.

3. Teach time management skills. Many of our kids are not able to judge time well. Consequently, "not now" means the same as "never" to them. Encourage them to include requests for specific information when they ask a question. In this way they can control the confusing or ambiguous answers we often give them. They like to know the details.

4. Help identify personal precipitators. This will be a very subjective list, with each element completely individualized for each child. This is a BIG step toward managing oncoming rage and learning to control it.

5. Help your child recognize his different levels of frustration.

6. Help identify personal stress relievers and practice using positive ones!

7. Seek accurate information and educate yourself about how your child's brain works because every person's neural

68

pattern is unique. People with brain disorders, like AS, often do unusual things, but knowledge will decrease the fear and confusion, both for the parent and the child. I remember the first time Kate realized that other people wiggled their fingers as she did. She was enormously relieved and felt as if someone had given her the right to do that. Her father and I decided that Kate was supposed to wiggle her fingers. She'd be broken if she didn't! You may think that's an exaggeration, but it's imperative that your child accepts his diagnosis if he is to live peacefully with it. Family acceptance and self-esteem will help the remainder of the world feel at peace with our children.

Good luck! You'll find solutions that work for you. I'm sure of it!!!

Infinity

Carousels and ferris wheels
go round and round with me.
And fans that come in many sorts
are always meant to be.
We Aspies we can spend our hours
watching things that go
around and round and up and down
repeating fast and slow.
It helps my thoughts and body, too,
to watch these things that spin;
'cause when my whole world looks at them,
my calmer self steps in.

By Martha Kate Downey
copyright 1999 *TAP DANCING in the night*

Silly Putty® and other stuff
Stress relievers for children

This list contains suggestions for both the child and the parent or caregiver. Some activities can be successfully used by a person of any age. If you think a technique is helping your child calm down (or keeping him from getting too "riled up," as my mother would say), keep in mind that your judgment is very subjective. You can't know for sure how your child is feeling inside. Remember that how he feels on the inside may not match his outward appearance. You may be pleased with the result, but the child may feel much differently.

1. Learn breathing techniques that are relaxing.

2. Do something physical and fun, such as jumping on a trampoline, running or jogging. Non-competitive exercise can also combat the tendency to withdraw into depression.

3. Get extra rest.

4. Practice proper nutrition. Try a small, high-protein snack (peanut butter sandwich) to calm a "wild child."

5. Gather resources and information about a new situation. Think through a scenario to determine how it might play out. Get information from someone who has been to the event or place before. This preparation helps a person feel more in control, better prepared and less frightened in a new situation.

6. Pack comfort items. Ideas include a blanket, toy, book, music, lacing cards, etc. Items should offer familiarity and comfort and provide a sense of normalcy for a new or scary situation. Showering, bathing, watching television and sleeping are activities that can soothe and calm in a home setting.

7. Maintain regularity of diet, schedule, people and sensory issues. This may be difficult to do during a crisis or times of high activity (such as holidays) but helps to maintain a sense of balance and control.

8. Use alternate ways of expressing stress or need, such as verbal problem solving, facial expression flashcards, masks, sign language, etc.

9. Allow for time. Sometimes anger just has to wear off, and the passage of time lets the strong pain subside. The voice of reason may be able to sneak in and whisper a bit of understanding.

10. Engage in something creative: artwork, music and dancing are a few choices. Drawing pictures could be a stress reliever. You could offer to show the picture to the person your child is angry at or just use the method for cooling down.

11. Permit perseverating when the behavior does not adversely affect another person or situation. Allow the use of an appropriate or agreed upon tic or stim without fear of retribution or condescension. Chewing on a toy pretzel, playing with a rubber ball, handling Silly Putty®, jewelry, beads or a balloon filled with flour are favorite comfort items to siphon off the physical need to channel energy. This can provide a calming effect, or "grounding."

12. Engage in a disciplined physical activity such as martial arts. Be selective about the type of martial art and class instructor.

13. Spend time with a "comfort person" who can support you, such as an aide, trusted friend or family member.

14. Hold something small in your hand that cannot hurt if thrown or handled, i.e. a piece of paper, tissue.

My Song

I hum, you frown.
I wave my hands
And you scowl.
My hands and body in movement
Create a calming sense for me,
But in your ignorance
Or need for "normality"
You try to stop my actions.
My very personal habits are not intended to distract you
Or irritate you. Nonetheless, you are even more compelled
To stop my body and mind from functioning in its very natural
way
Than I am compelled to practice my self-stimulating habits.
Why is it that what relaxes me - irritates you?
Maybe you should try it!
If your mind were less afraid and more open,
Could you not see that my body is simply doing its own dance?
Singing its own song?

by Martha Kate Downey
****

By Martha Kate Downey
copyright 1999 *TAP DANCING in the night*

What can I do as a parent?

I know there are many suggestions in this book for parents who care for children with special needs. To do ALL those things would be impossible. The following suggestions are NOT offered as a "to do" list, but rather as ideas that might help ease the tension or solve a problem in your household. The trick is to identify possible stressors for your child, then apply the most beneficial problem-solving techniques.

1. Give examples of appropriate and inappropriate ways to vent anger. By sharing your own effective methods of handling frustrations and disappointment, your child will learn skills and better understand family expectations. Make sure you are practicing what you preach! This is SO hard!

2. Be clear and realistic about expectations.

3. Give very clear instructions. Be as calm and direct as possible, repeating or rephrasing instructions as needed.

    A. Make sure you have your child's attention.
    B. Speak more slowly than usual.
    C. Use short sentences.
    D. Make physical contact while talking with the child, unless he is sensory defensive.
    E. Ask him if he understood what you said. Watch for signs of mimic behavior without comprehension. Have the child *reword*, NOT *repeat* your instructions.

4. Speak as softly as possible when giving instructions.

Have any of you heard Bill Cosby's comedy routine that includes the bit about kids and whispering? Ambling across the stage, Cosby rolls his eyes and attests to the fact that if you speak loudly to tell your kids to do something, or NOT to do something, they can't "hear" you. But whisper "candy" or "money" and you've got the undivided attention of every child in the house! Sounds a bit like my friend, Anne, who complains, "No matter how many times I yell at my kids to clear their dishes or walk the dog, they play dumb and act like they've got cotton in their ears. I mean, what could be more important than throwing popcorn at your sister while she watches an after school cartoon for the twelfth time? But the minute I casually stroll into the room and imperceptibly whisper, 'I'll pay ten bucks to wash the car,' you've got your kids, the neighbor's kids and all their friends clamoring for a wet sponge!"
I personally don't know about kids and wet sponges, but do know that everyone in the house hears me if I open a sack of Oreos in the privacy of my own closet!
MK

5. Pick your battles. Set priorities. If there are many skills you would like to help your child work on, don't attempt to teach them all at the same time. Begin with one that the child may easily accomplish, or a not-so-good habit you might easily nip in the bud or the one that is creating the most problems.

6. Rehearse anything new that might cause stress...anything from receiving an award to expectations for behavior at a funeral or circus.

7. Beware of holidays. Prepare for new situations and people beforehand. (Use the role-playing strategy.) Get as much rest before and during the celebration as possible. Schedule sufficient "chill out" time.

8. Prepare as much as possible for stressful situations or particular periods of the day. The 5 o'clock "witching hour" is especially stressful. School is over, supper hasn't started, everyone is hungry and cross, parents are trying to get things done, working parents are trying to unwind, stay-at-home parents are tired after a long day.... you get the idea. Things to try at 5pm:

   o Snack: peanut butter sandwiches worked wonders for Kate (the protein seemed to settle her right down). For others, celery and carrots with a small bowl of low-calorie salad dressing could be a quick snack.

   o Watching television, playing in a soapy sink or with the dog may help. The goal is to have a planned activity, not just random whining time. Sometimes a quick catnap can ease anxiety or frustration, but watch the clock. This doesn't work with every child. Napping may make for a more pleasant evening, but bedtime won't come quite so early.

9. Encourage your child to accept who he is. It is important for every child to feel proud of his own strengths and confident about his uniqueness.

10. Look for positive learning opportunities around you.

11. Be confident about your parenting style and decisions. It provides a sense of security for your children and increases their own self-confidence.

12. Work on your own willingness to be a "different parent" too. Normal is not good if it doesn't work! With your child's uniqueness comes the necessity for parenting skills and habits that are also unique. Be prepared: other people may not always appreciate your viewpoint or your parenting decisions. Locate support systems that will provide understanding and build confidence.

13. Teach your child how to admit his mistakes and work toward learning better skills by setting a good example yourself. Admitting our mistakes demonstrates strength of character and trustworthiness.

14. Remember that children will rise to your expectation, so keep it a positive one.

15. Speak well of your child when you know he's listening.

16. Be honest with yourself about who is in control. Realize that you may only provide guidance and act as a positive role model; you may not live his life *for* him.

17. Remember that a temper tantrum is not necessarily directed at you. I struggle to remember that sometimes (most times) my child's behavior has NOTHING to do with me. By acknowledging that we are not directly involved in every trial our child faces, we maintain a better sense of balance and are able to be more objective in our reasoning.

18. Be aware that facial expressions and behaviors may not reflect what's truly going on.

19. Help your child learn to identify facial expressions. Make sure your child is looking at the whole face, not just part of the face. Studies have shown that many of our kids look at the chin, mouth and one cheek but rarely focus on the eyes.

20. Be as tangible and specific as possible in relation to time concepts. "Later..." "After..." "In a little while..." all mean the same thing to your special needs child. Offer him tangible and specific information: "**When you get out of bed and eat breakfast**, then you may..." or "Yes, you may swing again **when we come back**." Vague phrases such as "Not right now" mean "NEVER" to many kids.

21. Practice cause/effect discipline. Explain the parameters to your child first, then take action or apply disciplinary measures immediately. An example could be, "Put the toy away now, so we may go to the park and play on the swings." For young children the choice and consequence need to be closely related in time (trip to the park is the imminent event) and context (playing *here* with the toy or *there* on the swings.) When you're sure the child understands, let him make the choice. Motivating with cause/effect discipline will help you determine if your child has difficulty with time concepts, task prioritizing or staying focused on a task. Consistent use of this type of discipline may help the child see why a task or change of activity is necessary.

22. Be careful if you use threatening language or ultimatums. Your child may choose the toy over the swing set so be

prepared to forgo the trip to the park! In other words, be careful what you promise. Make sure you're not just punishing yourself!

23. Work for the right school placement. Not all schools are the same. Consider a variety of options: private schools, other public school settings, special programs, homeschooling, etc. You may even want to consider relocating your residence if necessary.

24. Understand tests and assessments *and* their results. Don't leave a meeting or conference in confusion.

25. Be aware of foods and external stimuli that can affect behavior change.

26. Make requests for change in a positive way, rather than as a negative command. The request, "Please use your soft voice in the house," stated quietly will be much more effective than the loud command, "Quit shouting, NOW!" Requests for change succeed best when the direction is given prior to the circumstance where you want the behavior exhibited.

27. Don't take a tired child into a highly stressful or sensorial place.

28. The best opportunity for teaching is between the time of peak stress and before the child (or you!) forgets the problem. For optimal growth you need a motivated, yet calm student. If the child is dealing with sensorial issues, he is already neurologically over-stimulated. Present new material in a calm atmosphere if possible. It is ineffective to teach during times of over-stimulation or high emotions.

29. Be prepared to compromise. Demonstrate your willingness to take new information, process it and reformulate a plan. Using real life situations that involve your child is the best way I know to teach diplomacy.

30. Remember that what your child feels and what he says may not always correspond. When your child says, "NO!" or "I don't want to!" it generally means, "I don't know how," or "I don't remember how." Kate would stick her thumb in her mouth and put her head on the desk. I thought she was being obstinate, but over time I realized I was mistaken. She meant to convey that she was overwhelmed and didn't know how to successfully accomplish the task.

31. Be aware that your child will not necessarily share your confidence in her. Confidence is a concept that is steadily taught over time. It is related to how calmly a person can handle anger or disappointment and how easily he can dispel his own internal feelings of failure. Whether dealing with personal relationships or her ability to calculate math equations, Kate's steps toward mastery and confidence were learned the same way. When she showed a lack of confidence, we'd return to the first mastered step and have her repeat that one step, then move on. I'd stop her progress before we got to the more difficult ones and highlight her past successes before proceeding. When we got once more to the original trouble spot, I'd tell her we would do it together. (Here's a trick I discovered: do the task together so many times that the child is not only confident, but also bored.) Eventually, Kate was so tired of my slow methodical help that she would say, "I can do it myself, Mom!" We

learned not to expect complete success at the onset of teaching a skill. Our goal was to accomplish one small task thoroughly, before adding another. Sometimes she didn't want me to help; that's when I knew her confidence had returned.

32. Build on your child's confidence by reviewing his or her history. First, name things that were easy, that he wasn't afraid to tackle...then move on to things he did successfully but required a little more bravery...then things he had courage enough to try to master. I'd include all kinds of skills like learning to ride a bike, brushing teeth, writing in cursive, making a bed, swinging, multiplying, or meeting a new neighbor. Kate had mastered many tasks throughout her life but sometimes needed reminders to boost her confidence when attempting new skills.

33. Set a good example for how you handle teasing. Sometimes people tease as a way of honoring a trait about someone. "Oh, you only made an A-," probably meant, "I recognize how smart you are." Teasing can be a healthy way of acknowledging a potentially tense situation and show that you recognize the "problem" but accept it with good humor.

34. Use sign language or secret codes to convey social cues in public, thereby not embarrassing your child with overt correction. I can sign to Kate, *"not A"*, and she knows her behavior or topic of conversation is "not appropriate." If she is standing too close to someone, I can sign *"distance,"* and she knows to move back. We borrowed this trick from a gifted kindergarten teacher who used sign language in the classroom so she wouldn't disturb a roomful of working

students when she was helping an individual. The students also followed her example by asking for help, or permission to use the restroom in sign. I particularly liked using this strategy when Kate was across the room from me at church and behaving inappropriately. I could sign to her without causing embarrassment, and she knew to cease the activity.

35. Role-play frustrating situations and appropriate ways to handle them. You might try a short play with "What if your friend asked you to do... and you don't think you can? What would you do? What could you say?" Practice the scenario with your child by saying the agreed upon sentence, "I don't know how," or "Help me, please," or "Can you show me again?"

36. Try and find a way for both you and your child to succeed. Stay out of win/lose situations by negotiating or offering your child a choice. An example would be telling your child he must shower, but he could decide when.

37. As your child grows, involve him more in discussing his general needs and activities, but let him handle the specifics to the extent he is able. Your child must learn to identify his own needs, options and consequences that might arise from his decisions.

38. Grant in fantasy what you can't in reality.

"Can we move to Hawaii?" asks Kate.

"Sure," Mom replies. "By the way, we need to remember to put muumuus on our shopping list. Oh, and let's plant an oleander tree so we can wear fresh leis on the trip over. I think we should take Aunt Mary, because she could paint a picture of the flora and fauna there. I wonder if..."

With a grin, Kate asks, "Who will feed the cat? Cat's don't like Hawaii."

At this point you know your child realizes that this conversation is a game. The kid recognizes that you would like, in your heart, to always say, "Yes" but don't always have that choice. This sort of play helps a child differentiate between fantasy and reality. It helps him discover how imagery can focus and partially satisfy wishes. Most importantly, it allows the child to see that his requests are heard, understood and appreciated, even if they can't be granted.

39. Explain to your child how you make decisions. Be specific. Tell him the basis for your reasoning. This will help him with cause/effect logic and sequencing. Try to use examples that don't affect your child; they will be less emotionally charged.

40. Teach your child not to borrow rage. Neurologically typical children have a tendency to do this more than those who have autism. Autistic children often have difficulty with *Theory of Mind, a process that enables a person to empathize with another, or understand the meaning of language and actions in the same way as another person. In this case, the absence of Theory of Mind is a good thing because it becomes less likely that the child with autism will absorb feelings that were generated by another person. On the flip side, this absence sometimes makes it very difficult to motivate an autistic child. If it is important to the parent that a child cleans his room, but the kid sees no basis for it,

he will not absorb the parent's motivation. This is not a good thing when faced with issues such as feeling motivated to depart at a specific time, dress appropriately or use proper eating utensils during a social occasion.

41. Ask as many questions as needed until you're sure you understand your child's point of view. Be wary about assumptions.

42. Trust Kate's theory that the "worst disability is a bad attitude." Without a can-do spirit, nothing may be accomplished, regardless how high your IQ or great your resources.

43. Choose the Good in all things.

44. Some years are just hard. When those times come,
    A. Look for fun. Make sure you schedule it. Make it a priority!
    B. Remember that your young child is part of your life, but not your WHOLE life!
    C. Make a conscious effort to spend time with your own support system.

45. Avoid overwhelming the child.... remember that every good idea does not have to be acted upon.

46. Get appropriate medical care for yourself and for your child. Be willing to consider medication, if necessary.

46. Crawl in the closet with an *Oreo. Get support and make time for yourself.

Calling in the troops

Outside help such as social skills groups, education-based therapists, etc.

The following list includes personnel, resources and tools that parents may enlist to provide support for their specially challenged child.

1. Peer role models or mentors: Someone your child admires will often provide the extra incentive to maintain appropriate behavior in a variety of settings. Peer tutors or aides help ease the child into new situations and teach specific skills or behaviors for participating at such venues as Sunday school, the cinema, riding the bus, birthday parties, etc.

2. Occupational Therapists: OTs who work in school settings, hospital clinics or private homes facilitate fine motor skills training (handwriting, self-care dressing, toileting) and promote gross motor coordination.

3. Sensory Integration Therapists: Sensory Integration research has documented that SI therapy is most beneficial when a child is still in the early stages of brain development. If the problems have been caused or exacerbated by outside stimulation you might try using earplugs, a Walkman® or a learning carrell. Professionals that address sensory integration evaluation or therapy can be located by obtaining a referral from your local Autism Society.

4. Video games: If poor perceptual or motor skills are an issue, video games are a fun way to improve eye-hand coordination.

5. Literature: Social skills books are typically written for elementary age kids, but we've been able to adapt them pretty easily as the years go by.

6. Social skills training: When Kate was nine she attended very productive social skills classes to practice anger management skills in social settings. A social worker and an art therapist led the classes. They utilized group activities such as role-play, class projects and community field trips. It was helpful for classmates to view other kids with angry reactions. The class would discuss what precipitated the confrontation and role-play alternatives. Kate and I also used a book on social skills with her Girl Scouts Brownie troop one year. This wonderful book is entitled, *Social Skills Activities for Special Children, by Darlene Mannix, and I have used it for many years.

7. Family support groups: Find one or start one of your own.

8. Speech pathology instruction and/or language training: Public and private schools, as well as hospitals, offer speech services. Most insurance policies cover a portion of the cost if you have to pay for private services.

One of the most important skills a parent can develop and pass on to his child is the process of locating good resources. No parent can do everything alone. It is the healthy person who looks for help, not the sick nor the weak, for they hide. Teaching a child to find trustworthy and capable help is a valuable thing to do.

Who really is in control?

As parents, we sometimes think we should be in total control of our families and ourselves. Granted, we assume the responsibility to care for our children, but we cannot force a child to think or act in any way we would demand. Even if it were possible to do so, it would not only deny an individual's rights but would also limit that individual's strengths. Recognize that, in all actuality, the only person whom you can control is yourself. You may guide your child, but you cannot BE your child. You may set a good example, but not force him to copy your habits. We must allow each person to choose his own pathway if we are to live together peacefully.

With encouragement and support your child will develop his own methods for gaining confidence and feeling successful. Those successful feelings will give your child a sense of control over his own life. That sense of control will be a determining factor in your child's ability to exhibit positive behavior and conquer less productive behaviors.

Remember, if you didn't put the pressure on, you can't take it off! Each person has the right to find ways of honoring themselves unconditionally. Each person deserves a chance to find those places in their life where they may live peacefully and productively.

Glossary

Asperger's Syndrome (AS) - part of the autism spectrum. It is characterized by unusual language patterns and difficulty with understanding the thoughts and feelings of another person. Appropriate social interaction is significantly delayed. Hans Asperger first defined Asperger's Syndrome in 1943; however, the diagnosis was not used widely in the United States until the early 1990's.

Aspie - a pet name for a person with Asperger's Syndrome. The name "Aspie" was coined by some adults who have Asperger's Syndrome. They wanted a friendly way to refer to themselves and to indicate that they have AS. In this book, it is used to mean anyone who has characteristics similar to those of people with AS.

Auditory processing disorder - a physical hearing impairment that affects the brain's ability to separate meaningful sounds from less important background noises.

Autism Spectrum Disorders - (ASD) a term that includes autism and related disorders: Asperger's Syndrome (AS), High Functioning Autism (HFA), Pervasive Developmental Disorder (PDD), Pervasive Developmental Disorder – Not Otherwise Specified (PDD-NOS). Some people believe Attention Deficit with Hyperactivity Disorder (ADHD) falls within this spectrum.

Behavior modification - a method used to change or control behaviors by using rewards and consequences.

Bi-polar - a disorder of the brain marked by extreme changes in mood, energy, and behavior; also known as manic depression. Symptoms may present during infancy or early childhood, or may suddenly emerge in adolescence or adulthood. Resources: The Bipolar Child by Demitri Papolos; ISBN 0767903161; The Child and Adolescent Bipolar Foundation: http://www.bpkids.org/

Body language - messages that our bodies convey to someone else without the use of words, like looking at your feet when you are speaking to another person because you feel shy or nervous.

91

Carrell - a small enclosed area for study without interruption. **Not** a time-out box used for disciplinary reason, but a quiet area providing little distraction. Many children enjoy working in learning carrells.

Cognitive skills - thinking skills that include the ability to receive, process, analyze and understand information.

Compulsion - an irresistible, repeated, irrational impulse to perform a particular act or group of acts.

Crisis Support Network - details the Cycle of Violence. http://crisis-support.org/cycle.htm

Dexedrine - a medication used to help control Attention Deficit Disorder.

Echolalia - a repetition of what is said by other people as if echoing them; reciting a word or group of words over and over when speaking. It is sort of like a language tic and is not done on purpose.

Erratic - not consistent.

Expressive language - the ability to communicate thoughts and feelings through verbal speech, sign language, gestures or the written word.

Figures of speech, similes, parodies, allegories, myths - words or phrases used in a way that is different from their actual meaning. Those with autism have difficulty understanding many figures of speech, but once they learn the meanings, may become quite adept at making puns.

Flavorful - In this book the word "flavorful" is used in place of "disabled." The author, Martha Kate Downey, first used the word in the book, If you've ever wanted to crawl in the closet with an Oreo. The author does not see children who have extra challenges as being disabled but rather as coming in different flavors, and in the case of her daughter, "extra spicy." These children are truly the spice of life and provide variety and meaning to society.

High Functioning Autism (HFA) - part of the autism spectrum.

Inappropriate - something used or done at the wrong time or the wrong place. It doesn't mean good or bad.

Literal language - language that is concerned mainly with the facts; free from exaggeration or embellishment.

Meltdown - complete inability to function due to overwhelming stimulation of senses, emotions or responsibilities.

Neurological - having to do with the functions of the brain.

Neurologically Atypical - when your brain works a little differently than most other people's brains.

Neurologically Typical (NT) - a term used to indicate persons who do not have neurological challenges. Frequently used by those within the autism community to denote friends, relatives, etc. who are not on the autism spectrum.

Non-physical meltdown - occurs when a person is unable to function in a positive way. It is similar to the type of tantrum that is not for "show" or meant to manipulate. The person does not display physical aggression but may seem agitated, out of touch with his surroundings or unable to focus on a subject or conversation.

Obsession - when a person thinks about a subject all the time, even when they don't want to; a persistent, disturbing preoccupation with an unreasonable idea or feeling.

Obsessive-compulsive disorder (OCD) - an anxiety disorder where a person has recurrent and unwanted ideas or impulses (called obsessions) and an urge or compulsion to do something to relieve the discomfort caused by the obsession.

Occupational Therapist (OT) - a specialist who works to improve the development and use of fine motor (small muscle skills), gross motor (large muscle skills) and adaptive skills (those needed to function in daily life).

Oreo - a cookie. Used in some circles to denote a comfort food. Often eaten in a closet by the author and other parents while reading a cheap novel or a small book on parenting flavorful kids.

Perseveration - continuation of something (as in repetition of a word) usually to an exceptional degree or beyond a desired point; obsessive repetition of a behavior or thought.

Pervasive Developmental Disorder - Not Otherwise Specified (PDD-NOS) - part of the autism spectrum.

Physical Therapy (PT) - therapy designed to improve movement and function of the body. Therapy is tailored to meet individual needs.

Prosody - an individual's way of speaking, characterized by the speed of speech or the rhythm and intonation of a person's language.

Prosopagnosia - problems recognizing faces outside of a usual setting or known context.

Role-play - a method of preparing and practicing behavior that will be used at a later time.

Rote memory - the ability to remember something and repeat it mechanically or unthinkingly (exactly as it was seen or heard).

School issues - resources for classroom help: Addressing the Challenging Behavior of Children with High-Functioning Autism/Asperger Syndrome in the Classroom by Rebecca A. Moyes

Sensorial - issues pertaining to the senses: hearing, tasting, touching, seeing, smelling

Sensory Integration Disorders - impairments caused when the five senses of the body fail to transmit the right information. SI is caused by neurological malfunctions in the brain.

Sensory Integration Therapy (SI) - therapy that uses physical activities to help regulate an individual's responses to sensory input. Resources: The Out-Of-Sync Child: Recognizing and Coping ... by Carol St. Kranowitz; ISBN 0399523863

Sensory Defensiveness - a negative reaction to over-stimulation. One or more of the fives senses can be involved.

Social Skills Activities for Special Children - an excellent resource by Darlene and Tim Mannix. It contains 142 ready-to-use lessons with reproducible activity sheets to help children recognize and practice appropriate social skills both inside and outside the classroom. Publisher: The Center for Applied Research in Education, Professional Publishing West Nyack, New York 10995; 1993. Simon & Schuster, ISBN 0-87628-868-9

Stims - minor motor stimulations (stims) such as rocking, humming, tapping fingers, sucking and rubbing fingers in circles or on seams of clothing. Stimming releases excess energy and provides a calming effect for the person.

Stock phrase - a group of words commonly used to convey a single meaning.

Tactile - relating to the sense of touch.

Tics - involuntary face or body movements. People with Tourette and other syndromes have tics. Tics may make a person feel tired or cause muscular aches.

Theory of Mind (TOM) - a term used to define the perception of a person with autism. It is believed that persons within the autism spectrum do not have the ability to perceive how other people are feeling or what they are thinking. It seems to be the reason there is such difficulty with social skills.

Visual perception - the way your brain understands what your eyes see.